Cooking on a Budget

Ash Mahoney

Published by One Jacked Monkey, LLC, 2018.

While every precaution has been taken in the preparation of this book, the publisher assumes no responsibility for errors or omissions, or for damages resulting from the use of the information contained herein.

COOKING ON A BUDGET

First edition. April 25, 2018.

Copyright © 2018 Ash Mahoney.

ISBN: 978-1980932307

Written by Ash Mahoney.

Would you like more budget saving tips, tricks and insights? Also, would you like to have notifications on future advanced copies of my books, free promotions and more? Then, subscribe to my Budget Friendly Newsletter at http://eepurl.com/cY15Db.

Introduction

WHEN YOU'RE ON A BUDGET, it can be hard to figure out what to cook, how much to spend, and even how to eat three times a day. Eating healthy is a completely different challenge on top of it all, but budget cooking is possible. You can eat within your budget, the right amount, and in a healthy way if you follow the simple steps and tips in this report. Budget cooking doesn't have to be difficult, and you don't have to settle for low-quality or tasteless meals.

Pay Attention to Your Body

IT'S ABOUT WHAT YOUR body needs to survive and run well. Keep in mind some people run better on certain diets than others. If you run on a higher carbohydrate diet, then you need to use complex carbs as staples. Some people run better with a moderate carbohydrate diet, such as those higher in sugar and low on the glycemic index (i.e. fruit).

What Do You Run Best On?

KEEP A JOURNAL TO SEE what foods your body responds to. If a food doesn't agree with you, then cut it from your diet. It doesn't matter if it's an essential staple or something you've had since childhood. You must pay attention to your body's wants and needs. If not, then you'll spend more money trying to satisfy cravings, figuring out what sits well on your stomach, or even replacing food you simply don't want.

When paying attention to what your body does and doesn't let you eat, you can modify what you buy based on what you are able to eat. This is especially true if you know what your body doesn't react well to. You then know how to narrow down the grocery options. Look for coupons on what your stomach reacts well to, especially if your body tries to be temperamental. The food that works best you'll want to freeze so you don't run out during months when the prices are higher.

Start with Staples

THIS IS SOMETHING YOU'VE probably heard before. You may have gotten a grocery list with the staples on it, seen your mother pick them up, or even had to figure out what staples are without knowing exactly what this was called. Staples is what you need if you're on a budget or not, and they'll help to improve what you're eating each and every day if you know what to do with them. When dealing with staples, it isn't about what you want. It's about what will make your budget stretch, but the best part about staples is that they're versatile. Below you'll find the staples anyone should keep in their pantry.

- **Lentils:** Lentils are great if you want a quick stew or soup, and it'll help to supplement leftover roasted grains or vegetables.
- **Black Beans:** These are a great filler, and are even in some desserts. Keep in mind, you'll be spending less if you get your black beans either on sale or fresh. Canned black beans are higher in sodium and they cost more, too.
- **Rice:** It doesn't matter if it's white rice or brown rice as far as being a staple is concerned. However, brown rice is considered healthier. It can make a wonderful breakfast with almond milk and raisins, or a great base for a stir fry. Rice is versatile and a cheap option for various meals.
- **Eggs:** Everyone knows eggs are relatively cheap. You

can get a dozen for less than two dollars, and you can get them even cheaper if you buy in bulk. Fresh eggs often cost less too if you can find them from a local seller, which also makes them richer in nutrients and flavor. They can be used as a low cost protein, and they aren't just limited to being used in breakfast.
- **Oats:** Oats are less than a dollar a pound in most places, and can be used for baked goods or even breakfast.
- **Onions:** This underground stem adds flavor to most any dish. And, the variety of onions allows for a vast pallet of tastes. You can eat onions raw or cook them up in different ways for various dishes. You can add them to roasted vegetables, stir fry, or even eggs.
- **Pasta:** Be careful because it's easy to get tired of pasta, but having a bag is always helpful. Combine any meat or vegetables with pasta to make a simple and cheap meal.
- **Broth or Stock:** You can get bouillon cubes or a box of chicken stock for usually under a dollar, allowing you to add more taste and depth to your cooking. It can even help you to use less oil.
- **Potatoes:** Starches are important, and fresh potatoes are a great way to make sure you have a filler in your meal. They'll keep you full and happy, especially with the various ways you can cook them. You can boil them, bake them, fry them, or even mash them. If you do want to buy instant mashed potatoes, make sure you get the bulk deal and use it sparingly. You don't always need to buy flavored instant potatoes. Most flavors you can add yourself by adding a butter, garlic, salt and pepper.

Dealing with Meat

MEAT IS ONE OF THE first things you need to think about when planning your food budget. What really eats up your finances is meat because can be pricier. You should eat less meat overall if you want to stretch your budget. This doesn't mean you need to go vegetarian. You can still have meat in your diet, but you'll need to scale it back. You can just cook a smaller portion, replace it with other protein such as eggs, peanut butter or beans, or even use beans as a filler for some recipes.

If you want meat but don't want to buy in bulk, then try buying smaller packages of meat and stretching it with healthy filler such as oatmeal or even breadcrumbs. Are you looking for ground beef? Consider grinding it yourself to save a few bucks. No grinder? Then just ask the butcher to grind the meat for you. This will save you money overall. You can look for quick sales too, which are marked down because they're about to pass their sell by date. You can either use them by expiration date or freeze them for later use.

Cheaper cuts are another way to stretch your meat budget. You can always tenderize, braise or marinate more affordable cuts of meat. Marinades and meat tenderizers can be the secret to sparing money while enhancing flavor when on a budget. When you can, buy a family-sized pack even if you're only cooking for you. They'll cost less per pound, so portion out and freeze the meat if you don't want to use it all at once.

COOKING ON A BUDGET

Lean meats are going to surprise you by being the better buy as well. Sure, the fatty package of ground beef is less expensive by volume. However, you'll have more meat overall from the lean package once all the fat from the other cooks out.

For lunch meat, you'll want to see if you can buy the ends as well. Grocers often sell the ends cheaper than they would for a better cut. Some places sell meat at a lower price than others, so check around your town to see if there is a butcher or meat market. If there is someone who homesteads, then you might be able to find unusual meats for a cheaper price. Rabbits, ducks and geese are common meats to find fresh in many areas, so look around just like you would for sales.

When Buying Fruit

WHEN BUYING FRUIT ON a budget, many people think they should go directly to canned fruit. Canned fruit isn't healthy, and it isn't versatile. In short, buying canned fruit is a mistake, so look for fruit you can get on a budget. Your staple fruits would include bananas, oranges, apples, and even blueberries.

Other fruits include:

- **Pears:** Most of the time, pears average cost less than fifty cents a cup, and are full of fiber making them a healthy choice.
- **Honeydew:** This is another great fruit with a sweet taste most people don't think about. It usually costs less than sixty cents a cup.
- **Plums:** These are nutritional powerhouses, and they're sweet. Usually they cost under a dollar each if you buy them in season.
- **Watermelon:** The average cost is usually less than twenty-five cents a cup and have many antioxidants.

When Buying Vegetables

FRESH VEGETABLES ARE healthy, but it's tempting to get frozen packets or canned vegetables. It's even more tempting when you see a can of green beans costs less than a dollar. There are vegetables you can get fresh and cheap, but you need to know how to prepare them. You'll want to trade out vegetables that aren't in season, but one of the cheapest and versatile vegetables to buy is cabbage.

Bell peppers, spinach, kale, lettuce, and corn are cheap fresh vegetables you can buy locally. You may often pay more for fresh vegetables at a grocery store than you would at a local farmer's market. Many flea markets also have a small section of people selling fruits and vegetables at a cheaper price.

What to Buy & When

YOU ALREADY KNOW WHAT some of the most affordable vegetables and fruits are overall, but there is a season for everything. When you buy something out of season, you're guaranteed to pay more for it. Off-season produce has to be imported or grown under certain conditions giving farmers a lower yield. If you buy in-season and cook with fresh, local ingredients, then you're going to pay less for each portion. Even though you buy vegetables and fruit fresh, you can actually freeze it for later.

If you have spare cash and room in your freezer, freeze some great buys so you don't have to go without during off-season. You'll save more money in the long run. Growing season isn't a month long, so some months will overlap. This list isn't exhaustive and won't include every bit of produce. However, these selections are the least expensive, non-exotic options to keep you on a budget while eating fresh.

- **January:** Broccoli, Brussel Sprouts, Cabbage, Grapefruit, Kale, Leeks, Lemons, Parsnips, Rutabagas, Oranges, Tangelos, Tangerines, Turnips
- **February:** Kale, Leeks, Lemons, Oranges, Parsnips, Tangelos, Turnips, Rutabagas, Cauliflower, Grapefruit
- **March:** Leeks, Lettuce, Mushrooms, Brussel Sprouts, Artichokes, Broccoli, Pineapples, Rutabagas, Turnips, Radishes, Parsnip
- **April:** Artichokes, Broccoli, Cauliflower, Asparagus,

Lettuce, Leeks, Mushrooms, Radishes, Rhubarb, Spring Peas, Pineapple
- **May:** Strawberries, Swiss Chard, Zucchini, Spring Peas, Rhubarb, Pineapples, Radishes, Mangos, Okra, Cherries, Lettuce, Artichokes, Apricots, Asparagus
- **June:** Apricots, Blueberries, Cantaloupe, Cherries, Kiwi, Lettuce, Corn, Peaches, Mangos, Strawberries, Zucchini, Watermelon, Swiss Chard
- **July:** Blackberries, Blueberries, Apricots, Cantaloupe, Cucumbers, Green Beans, Corn, Kiwi, Lettuce, Okra, Peaches, Mangos, Peppers, Plums, Strawberries, Summer squash, Raspberries, Swiss Chard, Tomatoes, Zucchini, Watermelon
- **August:** Butternut Squash, Apricots, Acorn Squash, Apples, Blueberries, Corn, Cucumbers, Eggplant, Cantaloupe, Figs, Kiwi, Green Beans, Lettuce, Mangos, Okra, Peppers, Plumps, Peaches, Strawberries, Raspberries, Summer Squash, Swiss Chard, Watermelon, Winter Squash, Zucchini, Tomatoes
- **September:** Acorn Squash, Beets, Butternut Squash, Apples, Cantaloupe, Cauliflower, Figs, Grapes, Eggplant, Green Beans, Lettuce, Mushrooms, Peppers, Okra, Mangos, Pumpkins, Spinach, Sweet Potatoes, Tomatoes, Swiss Chard
- **October:** Beets, Broccoli, Brussel Sprouts, Butternut Squash, acorn Squash, Apples, Cabbage, Cranberries, Cauliflower, Leeks, Lettuce, Grapes, Mushrooms, Parsnips, Pumpkins, Rutabagas, Sweet Potatoes, Swiss Chard, Sweet Potatoes, Winter Squash, Turnips
- **November:** Cabbage, Cauliflower, Brussel Sprouts,

Beets, Broccoli, Cranberries, Leeks, Oranges, Pears, Parsnips, Leeks, Pumpkins, Sweet Potatoes, Tangerines, Turnips, Spinach, Winter Squash
- **December:** Broccoli, Cabbage, Grapefruit, Kale, Leeks, Mushrooms, Papayas, Oranges, Pears, Sweet Potatoes, Turnips, Tangerines, Cauliflower, Brussel Sprouts

The Importance of Herbs & Spices

WHEN YOU'RE COOKING on a budget, it's essential you don't get bored with what you cook. If you get bored with the ingredients you're using, then you'll be more tempted to break your budget or grow frustrated. This is less likely to happen if you use different herbs and spices to liven your food. It's the exact reason you should keep onions and broth as a pantry staple.

When you finally venture into the spice section of your grocery store, you'll be shocked by the difference in prices. You'll find budget garlic powder for under a dollar when another brand may ask for up to seven dollars for the same thing. Higher quality spices and herbs are going to be more expensive, but the quality difference is minimal. Basic grocery store spices are more than enough for most people.

You can even buy spices in bulk if you want to save more. The bigger shaker of salt and pepper is certainly something you'll use, so why not buy the bigger size? If you're worried about handling the bigger size, buy a smaller container to put it in. A small shaker will do wonders if you want to refill it. Here's a list of essential spices you'll want to keep stocked.

- Basil
- Garlic Powdered
- Minced Onion or Onion Powder
- Dill Weed
- Ground Ginger

- Oregano
- Thyme
- Salt
- Black Pepper
- Sage
- Paprika
- Rosemary
- Thyme
- Chili Powder
- Bay Leaves
- Ground Cinnamon

Still you may find you eat certain foods more than others. If you're eating the following cuisines, then try the spices below.

- **Italian:** Crushed Red Pepper, Italian Seasoning, Fennel
- **Mexican Cooking:** Cumin
- **Asian Cooking:** Curry Powder, Sesame Seed, Crushed Red Pepper
- **Baking:** Ground Cloves, Ground Nutmeg, Ground Allspice, Ground Cardamom, Poppy Seeds
- **Holiday Baking & Cooking:** Whole Allspice, Paprika, Poultry Seasoning, Sage, Summer Savories

Make Big Batches

BUYING FOOD IN BULK gives you better deals, but some people don't know what to do with all the food. Luckily, with a freezer you can make big batches. This doesn't mean you need to just cook large lasagnas, stews, and crockpot meals and freeze the rest. This is one way to do it, but it's not the only way. There's no reason to limit it to common meals. For example, if you buy ten pounds of onions, you may only need about one pound per day. Do you like caramelized onions? If so, then caramelize your other nine pounds, make them into small patties, and freeze them for later use.

This will even save you time later as well as cash. You can even just make big batches of meat. Get a multi-purpose type of meat such as chicken, pork shoulder, or roast and then cook it up. You can then portion it out, and leave some out to use. You can use this same method and do it with food you'd normally throw away. Maybe a bell pepper has a soft spot. Cut and separate bad spot from the bell pepper, and freeze it if you aren't going to use it right away. You can then add this to chili, eggs, or spaghetti. If your bananas are going bad, cut them up and freeze them for your morning cereal or even smoothies.

A Final Note

BUDGET COOKING ISN'T difficult unless you aren't selectively shopping. Make a habit of using coupons and buying food on sale. Look for coupons in your local paper and online. You may also find coupons for your local stores. Many grocers will let you combine coupons. If you get a manufacturer's coupon, then you can usually combine it with a store coupon. Shop smart and time-specific. Add these coupons on top of a sale price. Below you'll find a few more tips to follow.

- **Eat First:** Shop on a full stomach so you don't buy unnecessary items due to cravings.
- **Use Your Freezer:** Always freeze leftovers before they go bad.
- **Plan Ahead:** Plan meals ahead, and try to plan them around sales so you spend less on a weekly basis.
- **Package Your Own:** Package your own snacks, juices and treats. By purchasing the larger pack, you're saving money even when you add in the price of individual baggies and other packing materials.
- **Meal Prep:** Set a day aside for meal prep so you can stick with budget cooking and work with the bulk items you have.
- **Use a Calculator:** Shop with a calculator so you can add things up as you put them in your cart. This helps you stick to your budget and makes you more conscious of shopping decisions.

COOKING ON A BUDGET

- **Price Check:** Price check before you leave the house so you're shopping at a store giving you the best deals. You'll want to shop at multiple stores for different items if the sales are good enough.
- **Brands:** Don't always try to shop name brand. If you can't taste a difference between brands, then there's no reason to spend the money on a more expensive one.
- **Discount Stores:** You'll want to buy at discount grocery stores if you aren't hitting up a farmer's market or flea market. If you don't have a discount grocery store, then look for a discount produce store.

Now you know everything you need to shop and cook on a budget. Just make sure you apply these tips and put in the time you need to find the right stores, sales, coupons, and meal prep to stick to a budget-friendly diet.

Author Bio

———

ASH MAHONEY IS A FULL-time college student at Bowling Green State University and an aspiring author. Always looking for how to save money at home, Ash feels cooking on a budget and healthy eating on a budget don't have to be mutually exclusive. That's why Ash enjoys sharing ways to save money on groceries and other tips in his books. Catch his first release in the short read of Cooking on a Budget: A Short Read on Simple Strategies & Solutions that Work for Saving Money & Eating Healthy, available at every major online retailer!

———————

WOULD YOU LIKE MORE budget saving tips, tricks and insights? Also, would you like to have notifications on future advanced copies of my books, free promotions and more? Then, subscribe to my Budget Friendly Newsletter at http://eepurl.com/cY15Db.

Don't miss out!

Click the button below and you can sign up to receive emails whenever Ash Mahoney publishes a new book. There's no charge and no obligation.

https://books2read.com/r/B-A-SHCG-ZZNS

BOOKS 2 READ

Connecting independent readers to independent writers.

www.ingramcontent.com/pod-product-compliance
Lightning Source LLC
Chambersburg PA
CBHW031958240526
45464CB00024B/1372